Secrets

John Townsend

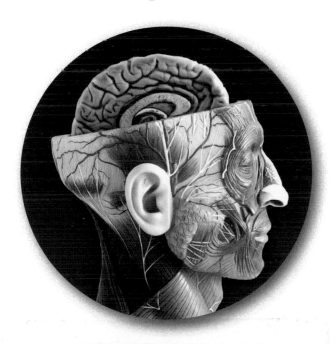

Badger Publishing Limited
Oldmedow Road,
Hardwick Industrial Estate,
King's Lynn PE30 4JJ
Telephone: 01438 791037

www.badgerlearning.co.uk

2 4 6 8 10 9 7 5 3 1

Gross Body Secrets ISBN 978-1-78147- 817-2

Publisher: Susan Ross
Senior Editor: Danny Pearson
Publishing Assistant: Claire Morgan
Designer: Fiona Grant
Series Consultant: Dee Reid

Photos: Cover Image: © Planet Observe/Photoshot
Page 4: © SB Photography/Alamy
Page 5: © Stocktrek Images, Inc./Alamy
Page 6: © BSIP SA/Alamy
Page 7: London Scientific Films/Oxford Scientific/Getty Images
Page 8: © Tom Wang/Alamy
Page 9: © BSIP SA/Alamy
Page 10: Nick Daly/Cultura/Getty Images
Page 12: Jonathan Hordle/REX
Page 13: © GeoPic/Alamy
Page 14: © Axel Hess/Alamy
Page 15: Jon Schulte/E+/Getty Images
Page 16: Matt Meadows/Photolibrary/Getty Images
Page 17: Stephanie Schuller/Science Photo Library/Getty Images
Page 18: SCIMAT/Science Photo Library
Page 20: Phanie Agency/REX
Page 21: Steve Gschmeissner/Science Photo Library/Getty Images
Page 22: © incamerastock/Alamy
Page 23: © defun/iStock
Page 24: Betsy Dupuis/E+/Getty Images
Page 25: © Maximilian Weinzierl/Alamy
Page 26: © gvictoria/iStock
Page 27: © Daniel Waschnig/Alamy
Page 29: © Eldad Carin/iStock
Page 30: © Nature Picture Library/Alamy

Attempts to contact all copyright holders have been made.
If any omitted would care to contact Badger Learning, we will be happy to make appropriate arrangements.

Contents

Vocabulary

acid

acne

bacteria

centimetre

colon

glands

intestine

microscope

millimetre

stomach

1. Stomach secrets

Your body is amazing. It's a super-machine full of secrets. But some of the secrets are GROSS!

There are acids in your stomach that mash up all the food you eat. The acid is strong enough to wear away a metal nail!

Don't worry – the acid won't eat away your gut. You get a new stomach lining every three to four days.

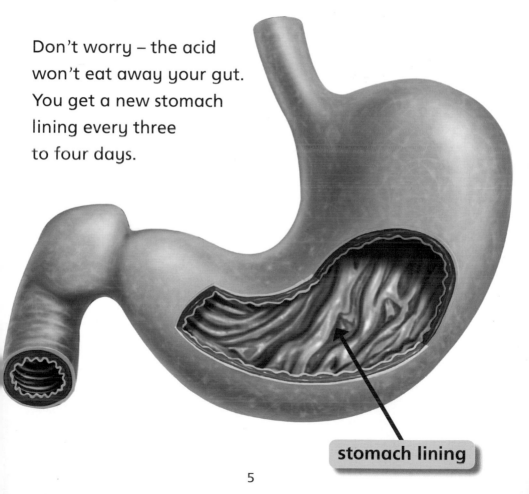

stomach lining

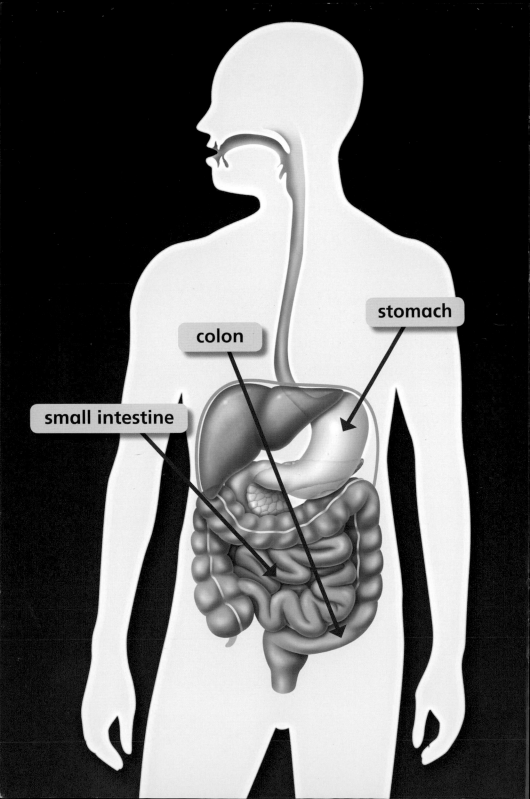

After being mashed and squeezed in the stomach, food goes into your small intestine, where all the goodness is taken out.

Then the leftover waste gets pushed along the colon and comes out as poo.

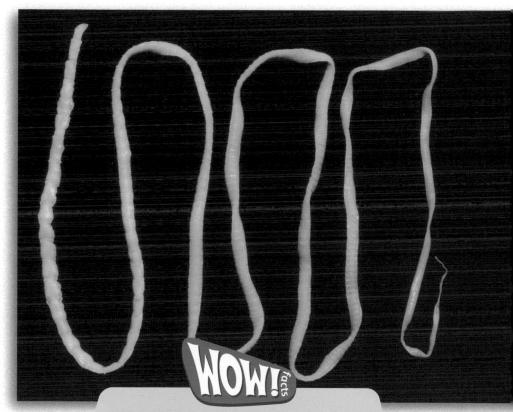

WOW! facts

A tapeworm can live in your gut for 20 years. It can grow up to ten metres long and you might not even know it's there!

Your bottom

Each day about ten litres of food and liquid goes through your body. Most of it is used to keep your body working. A small amount ends up as poo.

You might eat 45 tonnes of food in your lifetime - that's like nine elephants! You will make about 15 tonnes of poo - that's like three elephants!

WOW! facts

One in six mobile phones has traces of poo on it. GROSS!

2. Gassy secrets

Your body makes gas. Some of that gas puffs out of your mouth or your bottom.

Oops!

As you eat, drink and talk, you gulp down air. That 'gas' has to come back up again – as a burp. Most people burp 6 to 20 times a day.

Burp records

Longest	Who	Where
1 minute 13 seconds	**Michelle Forgione**	**Italy**

Loudest	Who	Where
110 decibels *(louder than a motorbike!)*	**Paul Hunn**	**UK**

Burping a baby helps to get rid of gas.

Bottom gas

As your food gets pushed down into your colon, it makes gas. The gas goes out of your bottom.

Your 'bottom gas' often makes a bit of a noise and smells gross.

Most people pass gas (fart) 10 to 18 times a day!

WOW! facts

Every day, the average person lets out enough gas by burping and farting to fill a balloon.

3. Yucky secrets

Ear wax

Inside your nose and ears are lots of hairs. Their job is to trap dirt, bugs and germs.

The wax in your ears may look gross – but it has a big job to do. It stops bad things getting into your ears.

Did you know? When you get stressed, you make more ear wax.

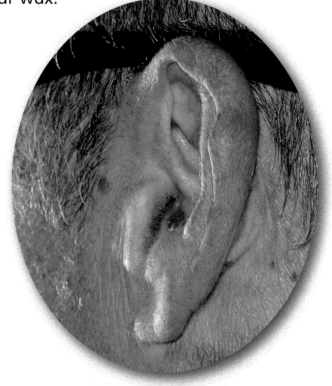

Ear wax can be yellow, orange, dark brown or
even black.

Snot

Snot is the yucky slime inside your nose. Your nose can make a cupful of snot every day – and when you have a cold it makes a lot more.

Snot stops dust and pollen getting into your lungs. When you breathe dry air into your nose, the snot dries to make bogies.

One out of every four people
picks their nose at least
once a day.

Joke

What's the difference between bogies and broccoli?

Kids don't eat broccoli!

Sneezes

How fast does the snot go? **100 miles an hour**

How far does the snot go? **10 metres**

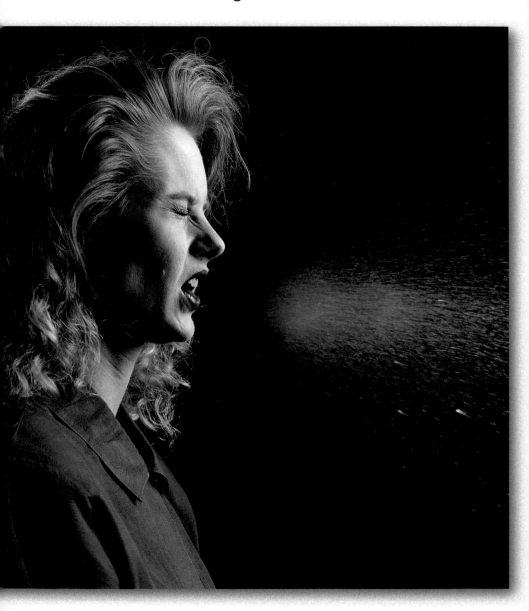

4. Bug secrets

Bacteria

Lots of things live on and inside you. Every square centimetre of your skin has at least a million bacteria on it.

There are lots more bacteria inside your body. Most of the bacteria don't harm you. Some bacteria in your gut help you digest food.

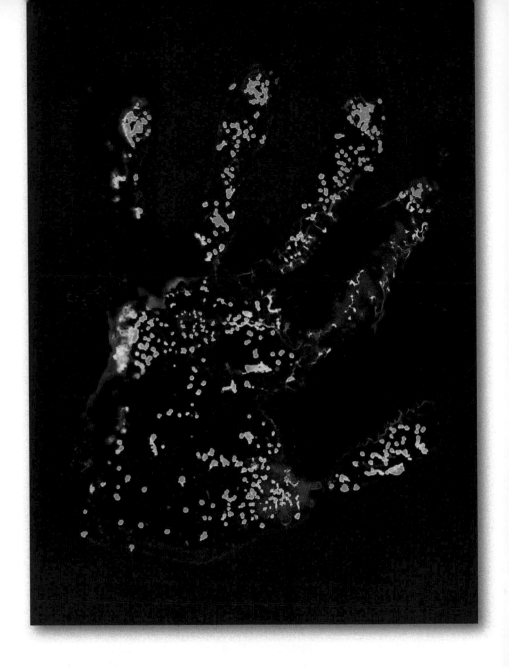

Hidden bacteria on your hand show up under special light.

WOW! facts

There are more bacteria in your mouth than there are people alive in the world!

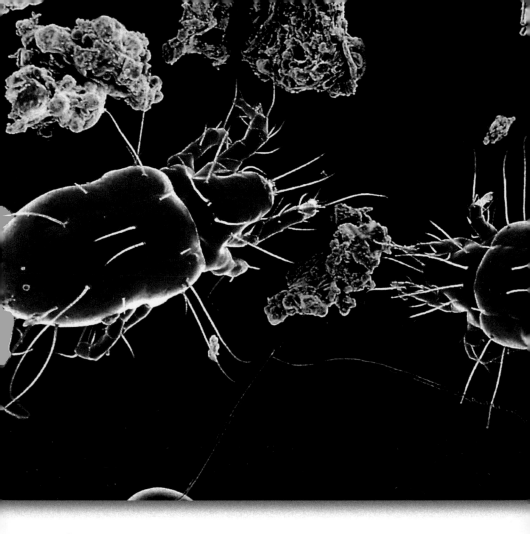

Mites

Mites are very tiny creatures with eight legs. They are too small to be seen without a microscope.

There are over a million dust mites in your bed right now. They are eating the dead skin cells that fell off you in the night. Nice!

Lots of people have eyelash mites.

These tiny creatures live on old skin cells on your eyelashes.

Eyelash mites are only a third of a millimetre long. If you put an eyelash under a microscope you might see one!

5. Oozy secrets

Blood

The blood pumping around your body keeps you alive.

If you cut your skin, blood oozes out. Then it clots to close up the wound.

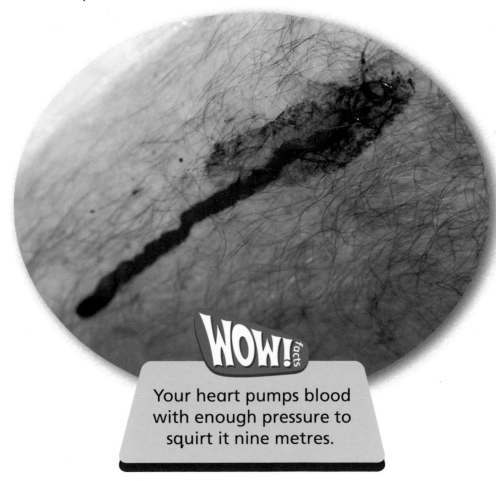

WOW! facts

Your heart pumps blood with enough pressure to squirt it nine metres.

A scab starts to form less than ten seconds after you cut yourself.

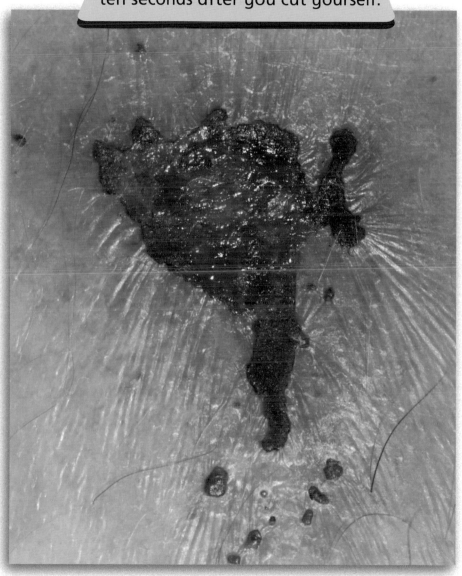

Some people faint at the sight of blood.

Pus

Have you had a cut that oozes white pus?

Have you squeezed a spot and out pops pus?

Pus is a mixture of your blood's white blood cells and bacteria. The white blood cells fight germs that try to get into your body.

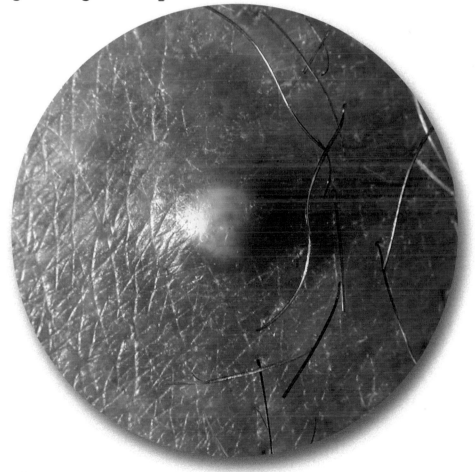

Sometimes the pores in your skin get blocked and you get red spots called acne. If pus oozes from a spot, the best thing to do is just to wipe it clean and give it a wash.

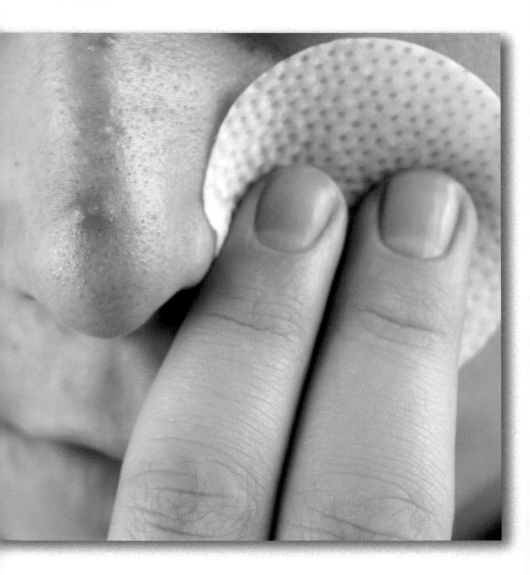

6. Sweaty secrets

Glands

You have three to four million sweat glands all over your body. The sweat helps to cool you down.

Bacteria can make sweat smelly so you need to keep your extra sweaty bits extra clean.

Every day you sweat about one litre.

1 litre

If you work hard, go running a lot or it's hot, you could sweat ten litres a day.

1 li... 1 litre 1 litre 1 litre 1 litre 1 litre

Skin

Every hour, over 40,000 dead skin cells fall off your body.

Every year you shed three kilograms of dead skin (that's like three bags of sugar). Trillions of dust mites live in your home and eat all that dead skin. YUM!

The dust in your home is mostly made of dead skin cells. GROSS!

The shed skin of a ladder snake

Some animals shed their skin all at once.

Questions

How often do you get a new stomach lining? *(page 5)*

What is scary about a tapeworm? *(page 7)*

How many times a day do most people fart? *(page 11)*

How fast does snot go when you sneeze? *(page 16)*

What is pus made of? *(page 25)*

How many sweat glands do you have? *(page 27)*

Index